STONE PAINTING FOR COMPLETE BEGINNERS

The Pictorial Guide on How to Create and Make Stone Painting Designs and Patterns from Scratch at Home Including Rock Painting Tools, Materials and Projects

Derrick Powell

TABLE OF CONTENT

CHAPTER 1

INTRODUCTION

Following the replacement of my old one-piece range with new equipment, I was left with a large expanse of drywall that needed to be completed. After considering my alternatives and deciding that I didn't like for most of them, I chose to paint a faux stone wall. Generally speaking, I am pleased with the outcome, and even more importantly, so is my family.

The first step is to create a plan.
Before You Begin Painting

Before you begin, please keep the following points in mind:

Thoroughly clean the surrounding area. Grit and webs will contaminate your paint if they get into it.

If at all feasible, paint before permanently installing permanent appliances or furnishings.

Make use of a base coat paint that is also a primer for the first layer.

Colors and hues may be created by combining the colors you currently have.

Colors and methods should be tested on areas that will not be seen.

Always keep a bucket of clean water and a cloth on hand!

CHAPTER 2

FAUX STONE PAINTING

Step 2: The Supplies You'll Need

Paint for the house that is good. Choose your finish, whether it's for the inside or the outside, as well as numerous colors. A minimum of one background color, one highlight color, and one contrasting color for the grout will be required for this project. Rust, off white, gray, and tan were the colors I selected for sample sizes.

A normal sponge will suffice.

A sponge from the sea

For big areas, use one medium-sized paintbrush.

Smaller brushes are used for fine details.

Pencil and eraser are provided.

a dish of pure drinking water

Paper towels or rags

Varnish is an option.

Step 3: Applying Paint on the Stone

1) Draw a rough sketch of your idea on the wall with a pencil. Simply sketch in the shapes of freeform stones. A ruler and/or painter's tape can be used to create brick patterns or angular shapes. Make the grout about a half-inch broad overall.

2) Paint the base color of all of the stones with the same color. Don't be concerned about being flawless. When you paint the grout, you'll be able to make the lines more precise. Allow to dry.

3. Use the sea sponge to dab a small amount of the highlight color onto your bricks. Work in tiny chunks at a time.

4) When the highlight paint is nearly dry, use a moist normal sponge and gently rub it in small circles over the surface of the paint. This will help to disperse some of the accent color and make the stone appear more natural.

Step 4: Create rough sketches

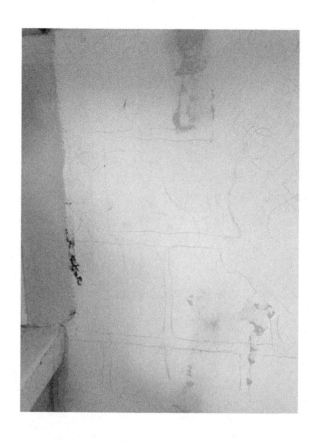

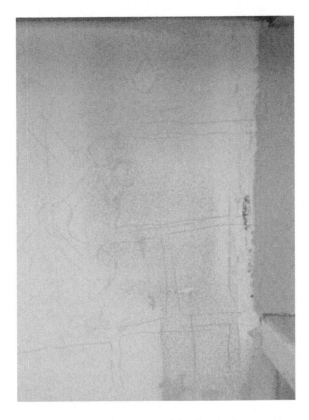

These are the initial sketches that I created. I simply happened to come across them on my phone and thought I'd share them with you. (I had initially planned to paint a trellis, but I changed my mind after some consideration.)

Adding the Grout in Step 5

5) Repeat the process until all of the stones are highlighted. Allow to dry.

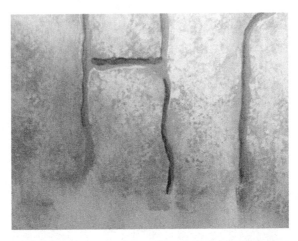

6) Fill in all of the gaps between the stones with your grout color. Allow to dry.

When painting each stone, paint a dark line (shadow) on one side and the bottom of each stone if you want them to seem more realistically. In addition, you may paint a highlight in a brighter color than the grout opposite the black lines to draw attention to them. Make use of a little round paintbrush for this. Allow to dry.

Step 6: Putting the Finish on the Wall

8) Create light and dark glazes (transparent paint) by diluting one light and one dark paint color with water and mixing them together. Test the glazes on an inconspicuous part of your body.

9) Using your sponges, paint the glazes on in a haphazard fashion. This will give the piece more depth. Remove everything

that you don't like. Remove any extra paint using a paper towel.

10) Retouch any areas that require attention and allow to dry completely.

11) If your painting will be subjected to a lot of wear and tear, you may want to apply three or four coats of varnish. (For example, a stove backsplash!)

Step 7: Make a list of all of the things you want to do.

CHAPTER 3

ROCK PAINTING STEP BY STEP

I am really thrilled to share this one-of-a-kind creation on Stone/Rock Painting with you. I purposefully picked this monochromatic pair of only the black over white and white over black to reflect and express a statement in a subtle manner. It is important to remember that the aesthetics and design elements are not sacrificed. While the lines convey a meaningful message, the stone/rock has been strategically positioned to pique the reader's interest and make him or her more anxious to discover what the message is.

I've created the perfect mix of two 'Good Morning' and 'Good Night' pebbles that are both cutely made. This is a basic and easy craft that requires only a few ingredients. Both the 'Good Morning' and the 'Good Night' rocks will be included in this project, and I will outline the procedures I used to complete each one. These pebbles might be used as paperweights or only for decorative reasons, depending on your preference.

2 Rocks are provided.

Acrylic Paints are a type of paint
that is used to create a variety
of effects (Black and White)

A paintbrush is a tool that is used to apply paint to a surface.

Pencil

Tooth-pick

Step 1: Prepare the 'White' Rock for Use.

I chose this rock for the 'Good morning' element of the project because it symbolizes the beginning of the day. Take a look at picture 1. To begin, I washed the stone/rock with soap and water and let it to dry in the open air for a couple of hours. Picture 2 shows a tiny brush being used to paint with white acrylic paint to create this effect. After completing this process, I let the granite to completely dry. This process usually takes a few hours to complete. Because this is a rock with a smooth surface, I felt it necessary to apply a second layer. This results in a finish that is smooth and consistent. After that, I wanted to do some freehand design work using a little toothpick or small stick, as illustrated in photos 3 - 11 of this post. You must exercise caution during this stage since the pattern will most likely spread if you were to accidently touch it. Attempting to wait for a few minutes before checking to see whether the pattern has been fully absorbed and settled on the surface, I failed.

Stone/rock painting is a somewhat more difficult challenge since the surface is not homogeneous and has a restricted range of colors. I used to get a thrill out of painting on a rock, but I quickly learned that it had its limitations.

As I proceeded to add designs on this little rock, I made a point of assessing if the placement of the designs was acceptable in order for the design to work effectively. Following the completion of the design, I chose to leave the rock hang in mid-air till the opposite side could be painted with a different creative arrangement. This side of the 'Good morning' rock was ready to be flipped over after a few hours of preparation.

Ready for Step 2: Preparation for the 'Good Morning' Side

I had strategically picked this
side for the 'Good Morning'
greeting since it was flat and the
letters would fit better in the
space available. This would
improve the readability of this
side and make it stand out on a
rock of this size and weight. I
did make an attempt to write
the words 'Good Morning' using

a pencil. Take a look at image 1. Then, with the use of a stick and acrylic paint, I free-handed the letters and added a tiny leaf at the bottom to finish it off. This appears to be really beautiful and well-organized. The next step was to let the stone/rock to cure completely before moving on. The paint is completely dry after a few hours. When both sides of the stone/rock have completely dried, the 'Good Morning' stone/rock is ready for usage.

Step 3: Prepare the 'Black' Rock for Action

Of the two rocks I have, this one is the darker of the two. This rock has a smooth surface and is significantly larger in size. It was agreed that I would use a dark hue for this since I wanted it to reflect the phrase "Good Night." This rock had a smaller, tomb-like surface, which made it more fascinating to paint on because it was smaller and tomb-like. I attempted to draw a design with a pencil, but the real work did not conform perfectly to the design I had drawn. In the end, I was able to complete a freehand pattern that would readily fit on this painting surface. When I was finished, I let the rock lie until it was completely dry.

Finished with the preparations for the "Good Night" side

The view from the other side of the black rock is shown here. This side was chosen because it has a more plain and level surface than the other. Due to the fact that there are letters on this side, it is critical to maintain proper spacing. To finish it off, I used a tiny stick and white acrylic paint to paint it. Refer to images 1 and 2. Allow this to dry fully before using. The black rock had been constructed on both sides and was ready to be used as a retaining wall.

CHAPTER 4

NAIL POLISH ROCK PAINTING

It's something I've wanted to do with my kid for a long time, and we finally found the time during summer vacation to sit down and do it. With the kids, it's a great activity to do together. Purchase a variety of vibrant nail polishes from a bargain store and have a blast painting stones. The nail polish dries rapidly and leaves a glossy, weatherproof finish on your nails. My son enjoys playing with the little brushes and brightly colored bottles. Small stones, on the other hand, are not recommended for usage by children under the age of five

since they might be swallowed
or stuck in their mouths. Do not
leave them alone or unattended.
You can gather stones on a river
bank or at the beach if you want
to save money.

Nail polishes in a variety of vivid
colors are available.

Stones

florets of broccoli

You can use any plant leaf of your choosing.

Step 1: Wash and disinfect the stones.

First and foremost, you must thoroughly clean the stones. It is necessary to clean up any filth.

Step 2: Allow the children to paint the stones.

Place the stones on paper plates or on a bed of newspaper. (Optional) Allow the children to paint the stones with the nail polishes. Their creations may include little creatures, paintings of buildings and sceneries, or simply having fun with different pattern combinations.

Step 3: Allow the Stones to Dry
Allow the stones to dry for a couple of minutes.

Step 4: Everything is ready to go.

The painted stones are ready to be used in a game.

THE END

Made in United States
Orlando, FL
30 July 2025

63396714R00030